Anonymous

The Lincoln and Hamlin Campaign Songster

The Continental Melodist

Anonymous

The Lincoln and Hamlin Campaign Songster
The Continental Melodist

ISBN/EAN: 9783337405106

Printed in Europe, USA, Canada, Australia, Japan

Cover: Foto ©Thomas Meinert / pixelio.de

More available books at **www.hansebooks.com**

THE
Lincoln and Hamlin
SONGSTER,
OR, THE
CONTINENTAL MELODIST,

COMPRISING

A choice collection of Original and Selected songs, in honor of the People's Candidates, Lincoln and Hamlin, and illustrative of the enthusiasm everywhere entertained for "Honest Old Abe," of Illinois, and the noble Hamlin of Maine.

FISHER & BROTHER,
No. 10 South Sixth St., Philadelphia; 64 Baltimore St., Baltimore.
Wm. J. Bunce, 68 Bowery, New York.

PREFACE.

In presenting this collection of original and selected songs to the public, the committee beg leave to say that they have endeavored to make it one that will commend itself not only to the political friends and admirers of " Honest Old Abe" and the noble Hamlin, but also to every lover of poetry and song.

The selections have not been made hastily or indiscriminately ; care has been taken that every thing that would be offensive to the most delicate mind should be avoided. In some instances it has been thought proper to soften unnecessarily harsh allusions, for which liberty the committee feel assured that, upon mature reflection on the part of the authors of the songs so interfered with, they will approve the motive which induced the alteration.

This collection has also the decided advantage over all other similar publications, in that every piece is set to a popular tune; thus rendering it particularly acceptable to Campaign Clubs and other political associations.

In concluding their labors, the committee beg leave to return their sincere thanks to the gentlemanly publishers and assistants of " *The City Journal*," for their kindness in furnish ing copies of some of the best songs in the collection.   CHAS. GITHENS, ⎫ *Committee*
L. C. REEVES, ⎬ *on*
W. D. MOORE. ⎭ *Publication.*

Philadelphia, July, 1860.

LINCOLN AND HAMLIN SONGSTER.

Honest Abe of the West.

AIR—"*Star-Spangled Banner.*"

BY E. C. STEDMAN.

O hark ! from the pine-crested hills of old Maine,
 Where the splendor first falls from the wings
  of the morning,
And away in the West, over river and plain,
 Rings out the grand anthem of liberty's warn-
  ing !
  From green-rolling prairie it swells to the sea,
  For the people have risen, victorious and free ;
They have chosen their leaders, and bravest and
  best
  Of them all is Old Abe, Honest Abe of the West !

The spirit that fought for the patriots of old,
 Has swept through the land and aroused us
  for ever ;
In the pure air of heaven a standard unfold,
 Fit to marshal us on to the sacred endeavor !
  Proudly the banner of freemen we bear :
  Noble the hopes that encircle it there !
And where battle is thickest we follow the crest
Of gallant Old Abe, Honest Abe of the West !

There's a triumph in urging a glorious cause,
 Though the hosts of the foe for a while may be
  stronger,
Pushing on for just rulers and holier laws,
 Till their lessening columns oppose us no longer.
  But o'er the loud pæan of men who have
  passed
  Through the struggles of years, and are vic-
  tors at last :

So forward the flag! leave to Heaven the rest,
And trust in Old Abe, Honest Abe of the West!

Lo! see the bright scroll of the future unfold!
Broad farms and fair cities shall crown our devotion;
Free Labor turn even the sands into gold,
And the links of her railways chain ocean to ocean;
Barges shall float on the dark river waves
With a wealth never wrung from the sinews of slaves;
And the chief, in whose rule all the land shall be blest,
Is our noble Old Abe, Honest Abe of the West!

Then on to the holy Republican strife!
And again, for a future as fair as the morning,
For the sake of that freedom more precious than life,
Ring out the grand anthem of Liberty's warning!
Lift the banner on high, while from mountain to plain,
The cheers of the people are sounded again;
Hurrah! for our cause—of all causes the best!
Hurrah! for Old Abe, Honest Abe of the West!

Rail Song.

AIR—"*Dandy Jim.*"

"The People," with unanimous voice,
For President have made their choice;
And the Fourth of March they will be able
To make clean sweep of the *Augean stable.*
So we'll cut and split and maul away,
At the Lincoln rails till election day.

Buchanan's "knees are weak" and limber,
Since the sudden fall of "*live oak timber;*"
Instead of ships with slave-trade sails,
We'll use the wood for *Homestead* rails.
    So we'll cut and split and maul away,
    At the Lincoln rails till election day.

And for this purpose the Keystone pledges
Twenty thousand mauls and wedges,
Now Loco-focos all, remember,
We'll split these rails by next November.
    So we'll cut and split and maul away,
    At the Lincoln rails till election day.

Then we'll secure Protective laws,
To keep our gold from Foreign claws;
From Border Ruffians we'll have no alarms
While freemen work their Homestead farms.
    So we'll cut and split and maul away,
    At the Lincoln rails till election day.

In October we will make this certain,
By hiding Foster behind the Curtin;
And in November you may rely,
We'll elect "Old Abe" and not half try.
    So we'll cut and split and maul away,
    And pile the rails on election day.

Up, Again for the Conflict.

BY WILLIAM H. BURLEIGH.

AIR.—"*Old Oaken Bucket.*"

Up again for the conflict! our banner fling out!
And rally around it with song and with shout!
Stout of heart, firm of hand, should the gallant
    boys be,
Who bear to the battle the flag of the Free!

Like our fathers, when Liberty calls to the
    strife,
They should pledge to her cause fortune, honor
    and life !   .
And follow wherever she beckons them on,
Till freedom exults in a victory won !
    Then fling out the banner, the old starry
      banner,
    The battle-torn banner that beckons us
      on !

They come from the hillside, they come from the
    glen—
From the streets thronged with traffic, and sur-
    ging with men ;
From loom and from ledger, from workshop and
    farm,   ·
The fearless of heart and the mighty of arm.
As the mountain-born torrents exultingly leap,
When their ice-fetters melt, to the breast of the
    deep ;
As the winds of the prairie, the waves of the sea,
They are coming—are coming—the Sons of the
    Free !
    Then fling out the banner, the old starry
      banner,
    The war-tattered banner, the Flag of the
      Free !

Our Leader is one who, with conquerless will,
Has climbed from the base to the brow of the
    hill ;
Undaunted in peril, unwavering in strife,
He has fought a good fight in the Battle of Life ;
And we trust him as one, come woe or come
    weal,
Is as firm as the rock and as true as the steel,
Right loyal and brave, with no stain on his crest ;
Then hurrah, boys, for honest "Old Abe of the
    West !"

And fling out your banner, the old starry
banner,
The signal of triumph for "Abe of the
West!"

The West, whose broad acres, from lake-shore to
sea,
Now wait for the harvest and home of the free!
Shall the dark tide of Slavery roll o'er the sod,
That Freedom makes bloom like the garden of
God?
The bread from our children be torn from our
mouth,
To feed the fierce dragon that preys on the South?
No, never! the trust which our Washington laid
On us for the future, shall ne'er be betrayed!
Then fling out the banner, the old starry
banner,
And on to the conflict with hearts undis-
mayed.

Hurrah for Old Abe of the West.

BY CYRUS ELDER.

AIR —" *Vive la companie.*"

Come all ye bold freemen and join in our song,
Hurrah for old Abe of the West!
While millions of voices the strain will prolong,
Hurrah for old Abe of the West!
Honest and pure is our champion's name,
Stainless his scutcheon and noble his fame,
Hurrah for old Abe, Hurrah for old Abe,
Hurrah for old Abe of the West.

Ye strong-handed yeomen now tilling the soil,
Hurrah for old Abe of the West!
Come chant the loud anthem, ye lovers of toil,
Hurrah for old Abe of the West!

Old Abe is the man who can work by your side,
He too was a farmer and that is his pride,
Hurrah for old Abe, Hurrah for old Abe,
    Hurrah for old Abe of the West!

And all ye who work in the mine and the mill,
    Hurrah for old Abe of the West!
Come raise your strong voices and shout with a
    will,
    Hurrah for old Abe of the West!
  He'll give you the boon of PROTECTION once
    more,
  He'll chase the grim spectre of Want from
    your door,
Hurrah for old Abe, Hurrah for old Abe,
    Hurrah for old Abe of the West!

Oh list to the notes of the loud bugle horn,
    Hurrah for old Abe of the West!
O'er river and mountain its echoes are borne,
    Hurrah for old Abe of the West!
  The cheers of the Boatmen are mixed with
    the strain,
  They're choosing old Abe for their captain
    again,
Hurrah for old Abe, Hurrah for old Abe,
    Hurrah for old Abe of the West!

The good and the pure and the learn'd of the
    land,
    Hurrah for old Abe of the West!
Have join'd our great army, and march hand in
    hand,
    Hurrah for old Abe of the West!
  They know that our Farmer and Boatman so
    true,
  Is an eloquent Statesmen and Patriot too,
Hurrah for old Abe, Hurrah for old Abe,
    Hurrah for old Abe of the West!

Soon murder and rapine no more we shall see,
    Hurrah for old Abe of the West!
The fair State of Kansas at last shall be free,
    Hurrah for old Abe of the West!
Her flowery fields for our sons he will save,
They ne'er shall be dyed by the blood of the
    slave,
Hurrah for old Abe, Hurrah for old Abe,
    Hurrah for old Abe of the West!

J. B. and his crew have about had their day,
    Hurrah for old Abe of the West!
They must pack up their traps and get out of
    the way,
    For HONEST OLD ABE of the West!
He is worthy to sit in Washington's chair,
And the true-hearted people are placing him
    there,
Hurrah for old Abe, Hurrah for old Abe,
    THREE CHEERS FOR OLD ABE OF THE WEST!

Campaign Song.

AIR —"*Rosin the Bow.*"

The Campaign commences most nobly,
    The battle has fairly begun,
And every new struggle proves doubly,
    That "BUCK" and his minions are done.

With the EAST and the WEST linked together,
    Our Candidate never can fail,
For the weight of a slave aint a feather,
    When Freeman get into the scale.

Every friend of our own "GALLANT HARRY,
    The STAR of the WEST," has declared,
The coming Election they'll carry,
    For every true man is prepared.

For "*Protection*" the Party will rally,
   "*Free Homes for the homeless*," as well,
Then we'll hear every mountain and valley,
   Ring forth to "FREE TRADE" its death-knell.

For LINCOLN the Party's united,
   And for HAMLIN the people are true,
The watch-fires all have been lighted,
   As once for "OLD TIPPECANOE."

Then bring out the music and banners,
   The "*Fence Rails*," and orators too,
And we'll teach Loco-focos good manners,
   As we did with "OLD TIPPECANOE."

Hail to our Chief.

BY A. AND H.

AIR—"*Hail to the Chief.*"

Hark to the voice from the broad prairie sweep-
    ing,
  O'er mountain and valley, across to the sea!
Dark Egypt arouses and wakes from her sleeping,
  To marshal her strength in the ranks of the
    free!
    Then, raise the joyous shout,
    Fling the broad banner out—
Safe with our leader our cause we may rest!
    While every hill and plain
    Sends up the shout again,
Hail to our chief—Honest Abe of the West!

Ever the faithful—wide known through the na-
    tion,
  From prairies of Texas to pine hills of Maine;
In cottage and workshop, on farm and planta-
    tion,
  They honor the statesman whose crest has no
    stain!

Tried in the race of life,
Nobly he bore the strife,
Hopeful and fearless, right onward he press'd!
Vermont and Wisconsin, then,
Send up the shout again—
Hail to our chief—Honest Abe of the West!

Sadly our watchword is heard in the " man-
sion;"
The Treasury vultures are quaking with dread,
Utah and Kansas, and slavery expansion,
Have finished Buchanan—his party is dead!
Cass, Cobb, and free-trade crew,
Thompson and Toucey, too,
Start, as the " thunder" breaks in on their rest!
Empire and Keystone, then,
Echo the shout again—
Hail to our chief—Honest Abe of the West!

Up, brothers, up! shall the horde of oppres-
sion,
Blight with their fetters our fair Western land!
No—safe from all bondage—a sacred possession,
For freemen and freedom, the prairies shall
stand!
Then be our battle cry,
Union and Liberty,
Victors or conquered, our cause is the best!
Bay State and Golden, then,
Sound the loud shout again—
Hail to our chief—Honest Abe of the West!

Old Abe.

AIR—"*Auld Lang Syne.*"

Old Abe was a pioneer,
His cabin in the wood;
He felled the trees, he shot the deer—
The work he did was good.

2

But other work is to be done,
    A wilder game to chase ;
A farm to clear at Washington,
    And Abram suits the place.
        Old Abe suits the place, ye men,
            He'll fill it with a grace ;
        Make way ! make way ! the people say,
            Old Abe wins the race.

A blacksmith, too, Old Abe was,
    A judge of iron he :
He holds that dear, which men make here,
    Not that brought o'er the sea.
And as he handles well the sledge,
    Wo to those laws which keep
Our wealth concealed in hill and field,
    For trade across the deep.
        Old Abe suits the work, ye men,
            He'll do it with a grace ;
        Make way ! make way ! the people say,
            Old Abe wins the race.

Old Abe is a mauler, friends,
    Good rails he always makes :
He'll fence the nation's treasury in,
    Full ten rails high with stakes.
No Buck will ever break them down,
    No Fowler find the prey ;
Go make the great Pacific road,
    He'll save the cash to pay.
        Old Abe suits the place. ye men,
            He'll give the vultures chase ;
        Make way ! make way ! the people say,
            Old Abe wins the race

Old Abe is a working-man,
    He knows the sons of toil ;
Nor thinks they should compete with slaves,
    Upon a virgin soil.

Old Abe is an honest man,
    All bribes he'll flee and shun ;
O what a curiosity
    He'll be at Washington !
        Old Abe suits the place, ye men,
          Behold his honest face ;
        Make way ! make way ! the people say,
        Old Abe wins the race.

People's Campaign Song.

BY CHARLES GITHENS.

[Dedicated to the " Continentals " of Phila.]

AIR—*" Nelly Gray."*

From Maine's distant valleys to the fair and fer-
    tile west,
    From golden California to the Lakes,
Hark ! how the notes are swelling from each
    patriotic breast,
    As from slumber each freeman awakes :
For the battle-hour draws near, and with hearts
    that know no fear,
    The People are rising in their might—
With brave Lincoln for their leader, th' bold
    Western Pioneer.
    Determin'd to conquer in the fight !

The cause is just and holy, and its aims and
    doctrines pure,
    The watchword, " Union, Peace, and Law ;"
The freedom which our fathers shed their life-
    drops to secure,
    The People are destined to restore :
There's glory in the fight, when we battle for the
    Right—
    Truth nerves th' arm—Justice strikes the
    blow !

Oppression and Corruption, and fell Treason's
    deadly blight,
Are the foes we seek to overthrow.

From the fair Eden-garden, where the prairie-
    lilies bloom,
Comes a blast that echoes loud and clear—
"Ho! gallant Pennsylvanians, with your West-
    ern brethren join,
And shout for our hardy pioneer!"
For the prairies are on fire, and each hardy son
    and sire
For the contest nerves his manly breast;
Their leader's brave and dauntless, and his name
    all hearts inspire—
'Tis Lincoln, the pride of the West!

By no slothful hours of dalliance has he won the
    path of fame—
By no lust of power and pelf allured;
Long familiar with hardships, and with peril, toil,
    and pain,
His worth its just mede has secured;
For he's honest, and he's pure, and all hearts he
    will secure,
The hour at length has found its man;
Each day new strength he gathers, while his foes
    grow pale and fewer,
As his worth and his virtues they scan.

Then success to the People, to the Cause, and
    the Man,
Shout loud for Home labor and Home's Friend;
To the flag of Protection, floating proudly in the
    van,
Free trade and its minions must bend!
Build the watch-fires on the hills, let the valleys
    and the rills
Re-echo loud a joyful strain;
Till vict'ry crowns the conqueror, and the Ruler's
    Chair he fills,
And the People triumphantly reign!

Freedom and Reform.

BY. F. A. B. SIMKINS.

AIR—"*We're a band of brothers.*"

Ho! ye men of every station,
Join with us for Reformation,
And for Freedom for the Nation,
   We're for Freedom and Reform.
     We're a band of freemen,
     We're a band of freemen,
     We're a band of freemen,
     We're for Freedom and Reform.

On the " sacred side " for ever,
We'll sustain " oppression " never,
But we'll go for " justice " ever,
   We're for Freedom and Reform.

We'll dry up disunion screechers
And wipe out the slave code teachers,
And cashier the slave-trade preachers,
   We're for Freedom and Reform.

We will oust the treasury robbers,
And the host of hireling fobbers,
And the horde of "live oak jobbers,"
   We're for Freedom and Reform.

With " Old Abe " to go before us,
And the flag of Freedom o'er us,
We will shout the sounding chorus,
   We're for Freedom and Reform.

Hurrah Song.

Old Abe's the boy to split a rail,
     Hurrah! Hurrah! Hurrah!
Beneath his blows the Locos quail,
     Hurrah! Hurrah! Hurrah!

He'll maul them just as sure as sin,
He'll pile them up and fence them in,
   Hurrah! Hurrah!
   Hurrah! Hurrah!
   Hurrah! Hurrah! Hurrah!

Old Uncle Abe's the people's choice,
    Hurrah! &c.
In him do Freemen all rejoice,
    Hurrah! &c.
It matters not what nag you back,
He'll win the day, so clear the track.
    Hurrah! &c.

Old Abe will make the " giant " fall,
    Hurrah! &c.
He'll beard the Douglas in his hall,
    Hurrah! &c.
Then let us write upon his crest
The " Giant Killer " of the West.
    Hurrah! &c.

The Democrats their fate bewail,
    Hurrah! &c.
Disunion's blast has rent their sail,
    Hurrah! &c.
By factions torn, they can't unite,
They fight for spoil—each wants a bite,
    Hurrah! &c.

They've fattened on the federal suck,
    Hurrah! &c.
But now are ruined by Old Buck,
    Hurrah! &c.
They've forced to travel t'other road,
Half scared to death at John Covode.
    Hurrah! &c.

Poor Bigler's in an awful sweat,
    Hurrah! &c.

And so is Yancey and B. Rhett,
>Hurrah! &c.
And Jerry Black is mighty sick,
For Schnable's at him with a stick.
>Hurrah! &c.

And if they do Disunion hatch,
>Hurrah! &c.
.Old Abe will bring them to the scratch,
>Hurrah! &c.
He'll hang them on the highest trees,
And prove that they're *weak in their knees.*
>Hurrah! &c.

Old Abe will guide the ship of State,
>Hurrah! &c.
Regardless of such traitors' fate;
>Hurrah! &c.
The Union flag unfurled he'll fling,
And to the nation peace will bring.
>Hurrah! &c.

Old honest Abe we'll call thee soon,
>Hurrah! &c.
To be our country's great Tycoon,
>Hurrah! &c.
For up Salt River Buck must go,
With Bigler, Yancey, Black & Co.

>Hurrah! &c.
But lest they there may lonesome be,
>Hurrah! &c.
We'll have to send beyond the sea,
>Hurrah! &c.
And bring them one to cheer their bones,
No other man than J. Glancey Jones.
>Hurrah! &c.

Lincoln and Liberty.

BY CHARLES GITHENS.

[Dedicated to the "Invincincibles."]

AIR—*"Hazel Dell."*

Hark! o'er ev'ry hill and dale are swelling,
    Anthems of the free!
The palace-hall and lowly dwelling
    Echo, "Liberty!"
Freedom's gallant sons at length are rousing
    From their lethargy;
The cause of Truth and Right espousing—
    "Lincoln and Liberty!"

CHORUS.

Freedom's clarion-notes are sounding
    Over land and sea;
From each patriot-heart the shout comes bound-
    ing—
    "Lincoln and Liberty!"

Too long have tyrant rulers blighted
    A land that should be free—
The hopes of patriot sires been slighted
    By tools of tyranny;
Shall the blood o'er Kansas plains once flowing
    Plead to us in vain?
Shall the soil in virgin beauty glowing
    Groan 'neath Slavery's chain?

CHORUS.

No! from mountain and from valley,
    Streamlet, lake, and sea,
Hosts of freemen to the rescue rally,
    For "Lincoln—Liberty!"

Soon their deeds with vict'ry'll be rewarded,
    The battle soon be won;
On Fame's bright scroll each name recorded,
    Clear as the noon-day sun;
On, freemen! upon the Right relying,
    Raise high each cheerful voice;

Let your watchword be, the foe defying.
      Lincoln, the people's choice!
            CHORUS.
Freedom's fire is brightly burning,
      In hearts once full of grief;
To the Patriot's Hope her sons are turning—
      Lincoln, our gallant chief!

Campaign Song.

[Dedicated to the Rail Splitters of the Twentieth Ward.]

AIR—" *Constitution and Guerriere.*"

Come, sons of Liberty,
      Ye generous, brave, and free,
In favor of Protection and the Union, O,
      Come, join the gallant band,
      Now forming through the land,
To aid the cause of Abe, the gallant boatman, O.

Old Buck, the "favorite son,"
      Has into ruin run
Our noble Country, through his reckless driv-
            ing, O,
      The People they are rising,
      (And it's not at all surprising,)
To aid the cause of Abe, the gallant boatman, O.

The Keystone State was sold,
      By the People being told,
To preserve the Union and the Constitution, O,
      They must vote for Buck and Breck,
      Who brought ruin, want, and wreck,
Upon our once beloved and happy Country, O.

They promised us Protection,
      And we've had it to perfection,

Just such as they intended for Mechanics, O.
   They now can laugh and grin,
   At the scrape they've got us in,
And how they fooled us with the cry of Tariff, O.

   Down in the Navy Yard,
   How nice they played their card,
Paying wages out to men to vote for Florence, O.
   But the thing is quite played out,
   For the People are about,
They'll shun *Thomas* with the greatest of abhor-
   ence, O.

   But the People's turn will come,
   And then you'll see some fun,
When these men before the Country, come for
   trial, O,
   Oh! how they'll squirm and squeal,
   When they begin to feel
The arm of Justice taking hold to crush them, O.

   To set our Country right,
   We're preparing for the fight,
In favor of Protection and the Union, O.
   Come, join our gallant band,
   And go with us heart and hand,
To aid the cause of Abe, the gallant boatman, O.

Our Glorious Constitution.

BY TOWNSEND HAINES.

Air—"*Tullochgorum.*"

Our country spreads out far and wide,
From mountain top to ocean's tide,
And mighty States lie side by side,
      In peaceful, happy union.
O'er all the borders wide and free,
        All our borders,
        All our borders,

O'er all our borders wide and free,
A noble, patriot band agree,
To guard their chartered liberty,
        Our glorious Constitution.

Our fathers gave the sacred scroll,
Wrenched from a despot's stern control,
With bloody hands, but noble soul,
        In dreadful revolution.
And cherished be its spotless page,
        And cherished be,
        And cherished be,
And cherished be its spotless page,
        While rivers run to ocean.
And cherished be its spotless page,
From faction and judicial rage,
As time rolls on from age to age,
        Our glorious Constitution.

Let demagogues exert their force,
To sway it from its destined course,
Its choicest social rights coerce,
        And spread around confusion.
Republicans in firm array,
        Republicans,
        Republicans,
Republicans in firm array,
Will right its wrongs—direct its way—
Instinctive will its laws obey,
        Our glorious Constitution.

What though the storms of strife arise,
And thunders roll along the skies,
And loud and fierce ascend the cries,
        Of treason and disunion,
With noble Lincoln, firm and true,
        Noble Lincoln,
        Noble Lincoln,

With noble Lincoln, firm and true,
　　　　　We fear no dissolution.
With noble Lincoln, firm and true,
To still the storm—the strife subdue,
The recreant shall his vow renew,
　　　　　T'our glorious Constitution.

Though traitors seek to rule the hour,
Like demons with malignant power,
And change a nation's richest dower,
　　　　　To haggard destitution,
We'll raise our banner broad and high,
　　　　　　Raise our banner,
　　　　　　Raise our banner,
We'll raise our banner broad and high,
　　　　　Inscribed with retribution.
We'll raise our banner broad and high,
And spread its stars along the sky,
And "sink or swim," and "live or die,"
　　　　　By our glorious Constitution.

Lincoln is the Word.

AIR.—"*Scots wha ha'.*"

[Written for the West Chester Wide Awake Club.]

Need we tell of others fame ?
We can shout Abe Lincoln's name !
His a tribute high may claim,
　　　　From each honest tongue.
Gather ! Gather ! in your might !
Who's the laggard in the fight ?
Ours is just—our cause is right—
　　　　" Lincoln " is the word.

Now's the time, and he's the man ;
Let the faction—let the clan
Strive to crush our noble plan—
　　　　For Human Liberty !

Strike for freedom and for home !
Falter not, success shall come ;
Soon shall foes be silent, dumb—
    "Lincoln" is the word.

Glorious stripes and brilliant stars—
Victor in the olden wars—
Fear we wounds, nor fear we scars,
    Our tried standard, thou.
Rally ! Rally ! in your might !
Who's the laggard in the fight ?
Ours is just, our cause is right ;
    "Lincoln" is the word !

Lincoln the Hope of the Nation.

"Dedicated to the Continentals" by

S. S. MONEY.

TUNE—"*Columbia's the gem of the ocean.*"

Oh ! Lincoln the hope of the nation,
The pride of the brave and the free ;
In the truth of a heartfelt oblation,
We offer full homage to thee—
Thy name as our watchword shall never
Be shrouded from liberty's view,
Oh ! Lincoln and Hamlin forever,
Three cheers for the brave and the true.

CHORUS :
    Three cheers for the brave and the true,
    Three cheers for the brave and the true—
    Oh ! Lincoln and Hamlin for ever,
    Three cheers for the brave and the true !

When faction is threat'ning the nation,
And dark clouds shut freedom from view,
The men for the hour and the station,
Are those who have ever been true ;

Then fling out our banner, and ever
Keep this our proud motto in view,
Oh ! Lincoln and Hamlin for ever,
Three cheers for the brave and the true.

CHORUS : Three cheers, &c.

A long and a strong pull together,
Will give us the leaders we crave :
In the fairest and foulest of weather,
We know they are tried, true and brave,
Then rally round them, and ever,
Keep this our proud motto in view,
Oh ! Lincoln and Hamlin for ever,
Three cheers for the brave and the true.

CHORUS : Three cheers, &c.

Fourth of July Lincoln and Hamlin Song.

BY CHAS. GITHENS.

[Dedicated to the "Continentals."]

AIR—*"Heart and Lute,"* or *" Auld Lang Syne."*

All honor to the patriot-band,
　Who in fair Freedom's name,
Arise to free our charter'd land
　From Tyranny's vile chain.
From ev'ry hill and plain is heard
　The war-cry of the free ;
As to the breeze the flag's unfurl'd
　That leads to victory !

Our brave forefathers fought and bled,
　Pour'd out their blood like rain,
That we in Freedom's paths might tread,
　Their legacy maintain.
Oh ! may the sons of honor'd sires
　Guard well the sacred boon ;
Long may the light from Freedom's fires
　Our glorious land illume !

But tyrants now despoil the land
  Where Freedom's martyrs bled;
Oppression still maintains its stand—
  Wrong rears its hydra-head.
But soon the hand of Justice stern,
  Grasping the sword of Might,
Shall from their thrones the despots spurn,
  Who Freedom's soil would blight!

Then onward march, like heroes brave,
  And boldly dare the fight;
Go forth to conquer, and to save,
  For Justice, Truth, and Right.
Your gleaming standards proudly wave
  O'er hill-top, vale, and sea;
With Lincoln bold, and Hamlin brave,
  Onward to victory!

Dug was once a Little Man.

AIR—"*Love was once a Little Boy.*"

Dug was once a little man;
        Heigh-ho, heigh-ho,
'Ere his shuffling tricks began;
        Heigh-ho, heigh-ho.
Little Dug was innocent,
Not, as now, on mischief bent,
Scheming to be President;
        Heigh-ho, heigh-ho.

Dug was soon a "giant" grown;
        Heigh-ho, heigh-ho,
With big notions puffed and blown;
        Heigh-ho, heigh-ho.
To strut and swagger he began,
Show a statesman, if you can,
To match this thundering little man;
        Heigh-ho, heigh-ho.

Dug would be a President;
        Heigh-ho, heigh-ho,
So his soul to treason lent;
        Heigh-ho, heigh-ho.
He broke a nation's compact through
To win the votes of Slavery's crew,
And kicked up his hullabaloo;
        ·Heigh-ho, heigh-ho.

Dug's career—is almost past;
        Heigh-ho, heigh-ho,
Though his mischief long will last;
        Heigh-ho, heigh-ho.
His name is now a jest and scoff,
The South—when he was worn enough—
Like an old shoe just kicked him off;
        Heigh-ho, heigh-ho.

Then let poor little Duggy go;
        Heigh-ho, heigh-ho,
But we must clip his wings you know;
        Heigh-ho, heigh-ho.
Oh! that so very small a thing,
Such misery and wrong should bring,
And a great nation's vitals, wring;
        Heigh-ho, heigh-ho.

Stevy Dug.

AIR—"*Uncle Ned.*"

Dere was a little man, and his name was Stevy
    Dug,
To de White House he long'd for to go,
But he had'nt any votes through de whole ob de
    Souf,
In de place where de votes ought to grow

CHORUS.—So it aint no use for to blow—
    Dat little game of brag wont'go;
    He can't get de vote, 'cause de tail
        ob his coat
    Is hung just a little too low.

His legs dey was short, but his speeches dey was
    long,
And nuffin but hisself could he see;
His principles was weak, but his *spirits* dey was
    strong,
For a thirsty little soul was he.

CHORUS.—So it aint no use for to blow, &c.

He could'nt sleep nights, for de nigger in de
    fence,
So his health it began for to fail,
And he suffered berry much from de 'fects ob de
    ride,
Dat he got on the Lincoln rail.

CHORUS.—So it aint no use for to blow, &c.

He shiver'd and he shook in de cold Norf blast,
And de wind from de Souf dat blew;
But de Locofoco ship hove him overboard at last;
So his friends had to all come to.

CHORUS.—So it aint no use for to blow, &c.

———

Song of the Freemen.

AIR—"*The Campbells are coming.*"

Ho! Freemen are coming—make room, make
    room!
Ho! Freemen are coming—make room, make
    room!

3*

With Lincoln to lead us, and Heaven to speed
  us—
Make room for the freemen—make room, make
  room!

Long, long have we yielded to wrong in its might,
No longer we're passive, but up for the right;
Where outrage and bloodshed run wild o'er the
  land,
We're bound to see justice dealt from a firm
  hand.
   Chorus—Ho! freemen, &c.

With Washington, Jefferson, and the true souls
Who fought where our banner its spangles un-
  rolls,
We've planted the white flag of sweet Liberty,
As the emblem of peace for the land of the free.
   Chorus—Ho! freemen, &c.

Then hurrah! clear the way, where our legions
  press on!
Humanity's with us—the battle's half won!
And over the battle-field, stainless with gore,
The anthem of freedom shall roll evermore!

Ho! ho! we are coming, from hill and from glen,
With " Freedom!" our watchword, and Freemen
  our men,
At our head the Rail Splitter; and proud be the
  day
When we chose him to lead us—ho! there—
  clear the way!
   Chorus—Ho! freemen, &c.

Clear the Way.
AIR—" *Home Again.*"

Clear the way! clear the way!
 Now, from shore to shore,
Shall glorious freedom's mighty sway,
 Be felt for evermore.

• From the northern granite hills,
    Far to the golden West,
The mighty cry for freedom fills
    Each patriotic breast.
       Chorus.—Clear the way! clear the way!

Clear the way! clear the way!
    Freedom's banner waves;
Our hosts are gathering for the fray,
    With traitors and with knaves.
Bold and brave, and fearless souls,
    Souls that must be free,
Resistlessly the torrent rolls,
    To glorious victory.
       Chorus.—Clear the way! clear the way!

Clear the way! clear the way!
    Brave men lead the van,
Lincoln never will betray,
    Desert—he never can.
On, then, on! nor fear, nor doubt,
    The banner forward bear,
'Till every wrong is rooted out,
    And Lincoln fills the chair.
Chorus.—Clear the way! clear the way!
       Now from shore to shore,
       Shall glorious freedom's mighty sway,
       Be known for ever more.

Campaign Song to the Wide-Awakes of Philadelphia.

TUNE—"*Yankee Doodle.*"

BY G. COLLINS.

Old Uncle Abe! long time ago,
    They said this to deride us;
But now we'll march to victory,
    And this's the time to guide us.

Old Uncle Abe! ha! ha! ha!
Old Uncle Abe, the honest;
How the frightened Locos run
From Uncle Abe the honest.

To fight is not a pleasant game,
But if we must, we'll do it;
As Uncle Abe began the fun,
His boys will see him through it.
Old Uncle Abe! ha! ha! ha!
Old Uncle Abe! the honest;
How the frightened Locos run
From Uncle Abe the honest!

Once upon the prairies broad,
Came a "giant" leader;
But Uncle Abe, with a cedar rail,
Soon made him a Seceder.
Old Uncle Abe! ha! ha! ha!
Old Uncle Abe the honest;
How the frightened Locos run
From Uncle Abe the honest.

Old Kentuck sent forth a man,
A "horse and alligator;"
But when he saw old honest Abe,
He did'nt like his cedar,
Old Uncle Abe! ha! ha! ha!
Old Uncle Abe the honest;
How the frightened Locos run
From Uncle Abe the honest.

Old Uncle Abe!—how it brings
The good old days before us!
Two or three begin to sing,
Millions join the chorus!
Old Uncle Abe! ha! ha! ha!
Old Uncle Abe the honest;
How the frightened Locos run
From Uncle Abe the honest.

Old Uncle Abe! not alone
The continent will hear it!
But all the world shall catch the tune,
And every tyrant fear it.

Old Uncle Abe! ha! ha! ha!
Old Uncle Abe the honest;
How the frightened Locos run
From Uncle Abe the honest!

The "Continental" Refrain.

BY LEMUEL C. REEVES.

AIR.—"*Ho! Boy's carry me 'long.*"

Ho! boys I'll sing you a song, it shall be merry,
 but true ;
These election times must have some rhymes, to
 help the parties go through ;
All up and down the land, they must fume full
 many a day,
To blow their horn, and mind their corn, and
 drive dull care away.
 CHORUS.—Ho! boys Lincoln's the man,
   Lincoln's the man for me,
 For Doug. and Breck. each other fight,
 So Lincoln's the man, you see.

Oh! Repealing Stephy Doug., your grave is wide
 and low,
You'll never get to the old white jug, but up
 Salt River must go,
Your party now is split—its platforms have the
 rot,
And there isn't now a party place where little
 Stephy may "squat."
 CHORUS.—Ho! boys Lincoln's the man, &c.

Oh! "it's a long "*Lane*" that has no turn,"
    and Breck. will find it out,
When Abe and Ham. to Washington come, and
    turn him right "about;"
And Breck. will say "good bye to all hopes of
    the White-House now,"
As he sees the honest old farmer take hold of
    the government plough.

    CHORUS.—Ho! boys, Lincoln's the man, &c.

Ho! boys a tariff we'll get, the idol of Henry
    Clay,
Then the sun of the people never will set, but
    shine through the whole of the day ;
On "Free Homes for Freemen" bet, and "Land
    for the Landless" as well,
And Lincoln into his cabinet will take "the
    patriot *Bell*."

    CHORUS.—Ho! boys, Lincoln's the man, &c.

Campaign Song.

BY A "CONTINENTAL."

AIR,—"*Dixey's Land*."

Here we are, as you diskiver,
All the way from old Salt River,
    Away, away, away, away. *Repeat.*

CHORUS.

We all go for Abe Lincoln,
    Away, away,
And when we get to Washington,
Oh! how we'll make the Locos run,
    Away, away,
    Away down South to Dixey,
    Away, away,
    Away down South to Dixey.

Oh ! we have laid a strong embargo,
On the Locos at Chicago,
      Away, away, away, away. *Repeat.*

We all go for Abe Lincoln, &c.

Oh ! now we'll have our little sport,
For the Locos have got very short,
      Away, away, away, away. *Repeat.*

We all go for Abe Lincoln, &c.

Now we are in for a good long race,
For the Locos have a very hard case
      Away, away, away, away. *Repeat.*

We all go for Abe Lincoln, &c.

Oh ! we can beat the Loco clan,
With our leader, William B. Mann.
      Away, away, away, away. *Repeat.*

We all go for Abe Lincoln, &c.

We all go in for Protection—
And we'll have it at the next election.
      Away, away, away, away. *Repeat.*

We all go for Abe Lincoln, &c.

We will elect Andy Curtin,
All the boys knows that is certain.
      Away, away, away, away. *Repeat.*

We all go for Abe Lincoln, &c.

We are the "Continental" boys,
Who fear no Locofoco noise.
      Away, away, away, away. *Repeat.*

We all go for Abe Lincoln, &c.

Campaign Song.

AIR—"Araby's Daughter."

Up with the flag ! let its broad folds float boldly
   O'er the land of our birth from the cliff to the
     sea !
Cheer it with full hearts that ne'er can throb
   coldly,
   When enemies threaten the home of the free !
"God and the right," be the watchword to
   cheer us,
   "God and the right," as we rush to the fray ;
Well may the foeman grow pale as they hear us
   Shout for the cause in our battle array !

We cringe to the lash of no Slavery's minion—
   We ask for no lessons such masters can teach ;
We hold to the right of each man's own opinion,
   We strive for free thinking, free labor, free
     speech—
Strive for the freedom our fathers before us
   Sought on these shores when they crossed the
     wild wave ;
With this for the motto to float proudly o'er us,
   We'll press to the contest that freedom to save

Remember, ye freemen ! the glorious story
   That tells how bold deeds for our country were
     done ;
Remember the days of her sorrow and glory—
   The glory that only through sorrow is won.
Let the long past with its memories golden—
   Let the rich promise the future may show—
Strengthen each arm and each true heart em-
   bolden,
   To rally together and conquer the foe !

———

Old Abe's Preliminary Visit to the White House.

AIR—"*Villikens and Dinah.*"

[The following song was written by Gen. Clarke, editor of the Burlington (Vt.) Times, and sung at a Lincoln and Hamlin ratification meeting at Burlington, at which the Hon. Geo. P. Marsh presided, by the "Bob-o'-link Glee Club."]

One Abr'am there was who lived out in the West,
Esteemed by his neighbors the wisest and best,
And you'll see, on a time, if you'll follow my ditty,
How he took a straight walk up to Washington
  City.
      Ri tu, &c.

His home was at Springfield, out in Illinois,
Where he'd long been the pride of the men and
  "the boys,"
But he left his white house with no sign of regret,
For he knew that the people had another to let,
      Ri tu, &c.

So Abr'am he trudged on to Washington straight,
And reached the White House through the avenue
  gate,
Old Buck and his cronies, (some chaps from the
  South,)
Sat round the East room, rather down in the
  mouth.
      Ri tu, &c.

Old Abe seized the knocker and gave such a
  thump,
Buck thought the State ship had run into a stump;
He trembled all over and turned deadly pale,
"That noise," said he, "must be made with a
  rail!"
      Ri tu, &c.

"Run Lewis, run Jerry, and open the door"—
And the "functionary" nearly fell down to the
  floor— 4

"There's only one man that knocks that way, I'm
    bless'd,
And he is that tarnal old Abe of the West."
                    Ri tu, &c.

The Cabinet, frightened, sat still in their seats,
While Abr'am, impatient, the rapping repeats,
"I hope it ain't Abe," said old Buck, pale and
    gray—
"If it is, boys, there'll be the devil to pay."
                    Ri tu, &c.

At last, though reluctant, Buck opened the door,
And found a chap waiting six feet three or four,
"I have come, my fine fellows," said Abe to the
    ring,
"To give you fair notice to vacate next spring."
                    Ri tu, &c.

"The people have watched you and made up
        their mind
That your management's running the country
        behind ;
You're badly in debt, and your plan is a bold
        one,—
To make a new debt to pay off an old one.
                    Ri tu, &c.

"You and Douglas have so split your party in
        twain
That Spaulding's best glue can't unite it again ;
And both parts are useless, the country don't
        need 'em—
For one goes for Slavery and the other 'gainst
        Freedom.
                    Ri tu, &c.

"So the people conclude that best thing to do,
Is to right the state ship, and hire a new crew,

And engage a new Captain as soon as they can,
And it is my duty to tell you that I am the man!"
Ri tu, &c.

"Come in," says old Buck, "and sit down Mr.
    Lincoln—
The remarks you have made are something to
    think on;
I don't care a cuss for the country, that's flat!
But if you'll beat Douglas you can take my old
    hat!" Ri tu, &c.

"Steve Douglas," said Abe, "he belongs in my
    State,
And I did beat him well in the year '58;
If I catch him again in the canvass he'll find
What it means when folks talk about 'running
    behind.'
Ri tu, &c.

"So you needn't fear Dug, let him scheme and
    conspire,—
He's as deep in the mud as you're in the mire,
And this moral he'll learn when his game is all
    played:
That it is not by 'squatting' that 'sovereigns'
    are made."
Ri tu, &c.

"Mr. Lincoln," says Buck, "your notions, I
    think,
Are extremely correct, and I ask you to drink;
We've the best of 'J. B.' 'green seal,' and old
    sherry,
And I've no great objection, just now to be
    merry."
Ri tu, &c.

Says Abr'am: "My friends, I've come here to say
That the Democrat 'dog' has just had his day;

The people have trusted you more than they
  oughter,
And all that I ask is a glass of cold water."
      Ri tu, &c.

"Cold water," said Buck, "we've got it I think,
Though 'tis not, with our party, a favorite drink;
Our tipple we take on its own naked merits,
And we need something strong to keep up our
  sperits."
      Ri tu, &c.

The Cabinet searched the White House with a will,
But did not find water "put down in the bill;"
Jerry Black made report that, without any doubt,
The whisky was plenty, but the water was out.
      Ri tu, &c.

So Abe took his leave and returned to the West,
Leaving Buck and his Cabinet somewhat de-
  pressed,
For they saw with a glance how 'twould end
  without fail;—
They were bound for Salt River, this time on a
  rail!
      Ri tu, &c.

————

John Anderson, my Jo, John.

A CAMPAIGN SONG.

John Anderson, my Jo, John,
 When we were first acquaent,
The "farms" of "Uncle Sam," John,
 For freedom's sons were meant.
But now the powers of slavery
 Have said it shan't be so;
I mourn I live to see this day,
 John Anderson, my Jo.

John Anderson, my Jo, John,
  When thou and I were young,
We hoped to get a farm, John,
  For ilka gallant son.
But the lands are gied to slavery
  Where can our bairns go?
O must they live in poverty,
  John Anderson, my Jo?

O dinna sab sa sair, dear wife,
  I bring ye joyful news;
"Old Honest Abe's" the man, dear wife,
  The people won't refuse—
He'll lead us on to victory,
  Triumphant o'er our foe;
The gallant sons of freedom's soil
  'Have sworn it shall be so!

The prairies i' the West, dear wife,
  To freedom shall be given;
The "old vile harlot, slavery,"
  Shall from free soil be driven!
Our boys shall get their farms, dear wife,
  And thou and I will go.
And tent their bairns' bairns, dear wife,
  Their lads and lassies too.

John Anderson, my Jo, John,
  Ye fill my heart wi' joy,
A farm upon the prairie, John,
  For lika darling boy!
"Old Abe" will help them split the rails
  To fence them in, ye know,
And ye ken they'll keep out slavery to,
  John Anderson, my Jo.

Lincoln and Hamlin Song.

AIR—"*Nothing Else to Do.*"

The war-drums are beating:
  Prepare for the fight!
The people are gathering
  In strength and in might;
Fling out your broad banner
  Against the blue sky,
With Lincoln and Hamlin
  We'll conquer or die.

The clarion is sounding
  From inland to shore;
Your sword and your lances
  Must slumber no more;
The slave-driving minions,
  See, see, how they fly!
With Lincoln and Hamlin
  We'll conquer or die.

March forth to the battle,
  All fearless and calm;
The strength of your spirit
  Throw into your arm;
With ballots for bullets,
  Let this be our cry:
With Lincoln and Hamlin
  We'll conquer or die.

Lincoln and Liberty.

BY E. HANNAFORD.

AIR.—"*Scots wha hæ wi' Wallace bled.*"

Freemen we! our freedom wrought
By our fathers' battles fought,
By our fathers' heart's blood bought:
  Freemen's sons are we!

Freemen we! and shall we stand,
Camly see the tyrant's hand
Stretching o'er all our native land—
    Death to liberty?

Freemen we!—and camly 'dure
Our blood-bought Freedom's forfeiture?
Witness daily more secure
    Tyranny become?
Freemen we! and ne'er oppose
The ruthless march of Freedom's foes?
While the tyrant's chains impose,
    At their back be dumb?

Freemen we! and by the blood
Of our fathers, which bedewed
The fields on which they Freedom wooed,
    On which they Freedom won.
Freeman we! by him who reigns,
The Freeman's God, and right maintains;
Vain shall be the tyrant's pains—
    Tyranny undone!

Freemen we! 'tis our's to dare
The battles brunt, and our's to bear;
Our's to wage, and know no fear,
    War of liberty!
Freemen, fight we—but no sword,
Not the sanguinary horde—
The ballot shall redress afford;
    There our victory!

Freemen we! hurrah! hurrah!
Gallant Lincoln well we know,
The people's friend, the tyrant's foe;
    Lincoln, Liberty!
Freemen we! press on! press on!
Work there is for every one:
The conquest urge, so well begun!
    Lincoln, victory!

Abe of Illinois.

AIR —" *Auld Lang Syne.*"

From many a freeman's home and hearth
  There comes a shout of joy,
(Who loves a soul of genuine worth,)
  For Abe, of Illinois.

No servile politician he—
  "True gold, without alloy ;"
Unanimous our vote will be
  For Abe, of Illinois.

No ! not for party—not for spoils
  Will he his gift employ,
But for his country's good will toil,
  "Old Abe," of Illinois.

Our hero once was short of pence,
  An humble farmer's boy,
We know he'll teach us how to "Fence—"
  "Old Abe," of Illinois.

To fence the Union all around
  He'll work—*he will not toy ;*
The cause is earnest and profound,
  For Abe, of Illinois.

Abe Lincoln Comes.

AIR—GREETING GLEE.—From the Minnehaha Glee Book.

We come with song and full of glee,
  From prairie wild and woodland free,
From hamlet lone, and city full,
  To swell with joy each patriot soul ;
And loud and long we'll swell the song,
  As on our way we march along,

And light each freeman's heart with flame,
   As we announce the favorite name.
Chorus—Old Abe Lincoln, Old Abe Lincoln,
     Old Abe Lincoln, Old Abe Lincoln,
     Old Abe Lincoln comes, he comes.

And Hamlin from the State of Maine,
   Who would not tarnish honest fame,
By voting for the Douglas bill
   Our western lands with Slaves to fill,
But 'mid that great pro-slavery broil,
   Stood for free labor and free soil,
Then to the breeze the banner fling,
   John Hamlin to the name we sing,
     Old Abe Lincoln, &c.

When Old Abe of the prairie State,
   Freedom's great champion in debate,
Met Douglas who threw open wide,
   Our infant States to slavery's tide,
What rapture fills the patriot's breast,
   As our great hero of the west
Beats down the wrongs, the giant quails
   Before the mauler of the rails,
     Old Abe Lincoln, &c.

Last fall when in the Buckeye State,
   The parties held a stern debate,
Douglas came down with chieftain's pride,
   To turn the scale on slavery's side;
But hearing soon of Lincoln's voice,
   He from necessity or choice,
Found business in some other place,
   He could not stand before the face
     Of Old Abe Lincoln, &c.

The nation's breast with joy expands,
   All hail, free men, free work, free lands,
Let freedom's fire be kindled free,
   On hill and vale, on plain and lea,

Let freedom's banner, wide unfurled,
  Proclaim to all men, all the world,
That highest on the roll of fame
    Shall be that honest, honored name,
      Old Abe Lincoln, &c.

Campaign Song.

[Dedicated to the "Continentals of Philadelphia."]

BY W. C. JOHNSTON.

AIR —"*New Jer-se-a.*"

Now, come awhile and listen,
  And don't be led astray ;
I'll soon enlighten you upon
  The topics of the day.
We're going to elect a President—
  For Lincoln we will try ;
For everything is lovely,
  And the *goose hangs high.*

Buck's honest (?) contractors
  He'll soon put to fight ;
We'll show them by our actions,
  We're battling for the right.
We insist upon home labor,
  And for a tariff high ;
Then the mechanic will feel **lovely,**
  And the *goose'll hang high.*

Corruption has been going
  About far enough,
Oh, Wm. B. Mann, he thought
  'Twas mighty rough ;
He brought the leaders up,
  And the Court it did them try ;
He sent them down below,
  Where the *goose hangs high* (?)

The Loco Foco party
  Is now completely split,
But Lincoln he will maul them,
  Until he gives them fits ;
We'll send him down to Washington,
  At least we will try,
Then Abe he will feel lovely,
  And his *goose will hang high.*

Oh, when we get to Washington,
  Then how we'll make them run,
And in their hurry leaving,
  You'll be sure to see some fun ;
With their baggage in their hands,
  Oh ! Lord, how they will fly,
And the CONTINENTALS will feel lovely,
  And their *goose'll hang high.*

The Restoration Party's Song.

AIR.—" *The Old Granite State.*"

O ! no more let compromises,
By such treacherous surprises,
And deceptive, false disguises,
  Be broken any more.

Chorus—We but seek the restoration
    Of true Freedom's ancient station,
    At the birth of this great nation,
    As fixed in eighty-seven.

All our captains and our leaders,
Will now boldly meet seceders,
And their host of special pleaders,
  Like brave, heroic men.
  We but seek, &c.

We will triumph this election,
Keeping Slavery in its section,
And give Freedom sure protection
    On Uncle Sam's domain.
      We but scek, &c.

All the sectional defying,
And upon the right relying,
We will keep our banners **flying**,
    Till victory is won.
      We but seek, &c.

Faith and Trust.

AIR—"*Zion.*"

Rallying round our standard bearer, ,
    March we to the battle field—
Ne'er unfurled was banner fairer,
    May it every freeman shield!
      On for freedom!
    Die we may, but never yield!

Long has insolent oppression,
    Revelled o'er our fair domain!
Rouse we now, a mighty nation,
    Freedom's blessing to regain!
      Strike for Freedom!
We will break the tyrant's chain!

Might is right alone in seeming,
    Justice yet will turn the scale—
Right is might—no idle dreaming,
    Press we on, we cannot fail!
      On for freedom!
Faith is strong, we must prevail!

Fearless are the chiefs who lead us,
Fearless too, ourselves must be !
We will aid them, while they need **us**,
But will bend nor back nor knee !
God of freedom !
We will bow alone to Thee !

———

Anti-Party Glee.

AIR—"*I once was Fond of a Social Glass.*"

I once was fond of party ties !
So was I ! (*3d v.*) So was I !
For in a name there's lots of noise,
That often drowns its nonsense.
The shouts and cheers were monstrous fine ;
Each party's praise was quite divine ;
But, you know well enough,
It was all mere stuff !
Exactly my case !
And mine ! (*3d v.*) And mine !

Then what's the use of leading-strings ;
When wire-pullers hold them ?
Why 'tis a piece of balderdash,
And that's just what I told them ?

I vote no longer for a name !
Neither do I ! (*1st v.*) Neither do I !
Pure principles are now my aim ;—
For worth and right I labor.
Though shouts for chains are monstrous fine,
Yet Freedom's shout is henceforth mine ;
And whate'er's the title,
I care precious little !
Exactly my case !
And mine ! (*1st v.*) And mine !

Then what's the use, &c.

I Spurn the Bribe.

WRITTEN BY ONE WHO COULD NOT BE BOUGHT.

TUNE.—"*Mountains, Farewell.*"

They knew that I was poor,
　And they thought that I was base,
And would readily endure
　To be covered with disgrace.
They judged me of their tribe,
　Who on dirty mammon dote ;
So they offered me a bribe
　For my vote, boys, my vote !
Oh. shame upon my BETTERS,
　Who would my conscience buy !
But shall I wear their fetters ?
　Not I, indeed, not I.

My vote ? it is not mine
　To do with as I will—
To cast, like pearls to swine,
　To these wallowers in ill ;
It is my country's due,
　And I'll give it as I can
To the honest and the true,
　Like a man, boys, a man !

Did I swallow down the hook
　That was baited by the base,
How could I dare to look
　My children in the face ?
Could I teach them the right way,
　While I heard a voice within,
Reproach me night and day,
　With my sin, boys, sin ?

No ! no ! I'll hold my vote
　As a treasure and a trust ;
My dishonor none shall quote,
　When I'm mingled with the dust.

And my children, when I'm gone,
Shall be strengthened by the thought,
That their father was not one
To be bought, boys, bought.

Campaign Song.

AIR—*"Auld Lang Syne."*

Come let's rejoice
With heart and voice,
Through all this happy land,
The friends of right
Are in their might,
Resolved to make a stand.

, CHORUS.

Resolved to make a stand, my boys,
Resolved to make a stand,
The friends of right
Are in their might,
Resolved to make a stand.

With Lincoln true,
And Hamlin, too,
We'll charge the foes of light,
The dastard band,
Can never stand
Against the power of right.

CHORUS

Against the power of right, my boys,
Against the power of right,
The dastard band,
,Can never stand,
Against the power of right.

Then roll along
The joyful song,

Let cannon loudly peal,
   Our honest aim,
   For aye the same,
Is our whole country's weal.

CHORUS.

Is our whole country's weal, my boys,
Is our whole country's weal,
   Our honest aim
   For aye the same,
Is our whole country's weal.

God made us Free.

AIR—"*America.*"

When Britain's tyrant hand
Spread darkness o'er the land,
   A dismal night—
The deeds by patriots done,
Heaven's benediction won—
God sent them Washington,
   And all was light.

The same kind hand appears
Through intervening years—
   'Tis God's own will.
Sedition's voice was heard
Threatening her hordes to gird,
When Jackson spoke the word,
   And all was still.

Now shall the people join,
When fiendish clans combine,
   To spread the blight,
Of Slavery through the realm—
Place Lincoln at the helm,
And faction's votaries whelm,
   In utter night.

Here then shall freedom bide,
And spread her mantle wide;
'Tis Heaven's decree;
And through all coming days,
Mingled with hymns of praise,
The undying shout we'll raise,
GOD MADE US FREE.

"Yaller Kiver" Melody.

AIR—*"Rosin the Bow."*

Come, all ye brave lads of old '40,
Who railed 'round Tippecanoe,
And give us your hearts and your voices
For Lincoln, the noble and true.

Come, show the whole world that our spirit
Is up again, "sartin and sure,"
And push right ahead for Abe Lincoln,
Good Abram—the honest and pure.

Come forth, one and all, to the battle,
Determined the country to save,
And strike for the jolly Flat-Boatman,
For Lincoln, the fearless and brave.

A bold leader is he to be proud of,
So now we will give him our best,
Then shout for the friend of Home Labor,
The patriot who hails from the West

For Protection he ever has struggled;
His coat you will find is home-made,
He goes dead against the starvation
That comes with one-sided Free Trade.

So for Home, and Home's friend, let us rally,
And never give over the fight,
'Till Old Buck and his honest contractors
Are put to inglorious flight.

We're engaged for the war, and we'll "go it,"
  You need'nt believe we'll back out,
For the flag of "The People" is flying,
  And Lincoln and Hamlin we'll shout.

Campaign Song.

AIR—*"Hurrah Chorus."*

For Lincoln now we sing our lay,
  Hurrah, hurrah, hurrah!
For he's the man, say what you may,
  Hurrah, hurrah, hurrah!
Now Illinois has one great son,
Who over the course swift will run,
  He is the man, an honest one,
  Oh, he's the man for me.

Old Abe can maul, or he can thrash,
  Hurrah, hurrah, hurrah!
He'll give it to your Loco trash,
  Hurrah, hurrah, hurrah!
Your two-faced man is naught to him,
E'en now his prospects are all dim,
  Abe is the man, an honest man,
  He is the man for me.

Abe is not rich in wordly goods,
  Oh no, oh no, oh no!
But in his thoughts, his works, his words,
  He's true, he's true, he's true.
'Tis he who loves his wife and friends,
And o'er his duty daily bends,
  He is the man, an honest man,
  He is the man for me.

Upon the Eagle he shall ride,
  Hurrah, hurrah, hurrah!
And of our nation be the pride.
  Hurrah, hurrah, hurrah!
While Douglas shall remain below,
And his own horn still have to blow.
  Abe is the man, an honest man,
  He is the man for me.

Campaign Song.

BY CHARLES GITHENS.

[Dedicated to the "Continentals."]

AIR —"*Dearest May.*"

Come, gather round me, freemen, some truths I
    will relate,
Of honest Abe Lincoln, the People's Candidate;
A man that's fit to guide the helm of our good
    Ship of State,
With pure and noble Hamlin—a good and worthy
    mate!

CHORUS:

  Hurrah! hurrah! for Honest Abe, hurrah!
      Hark! how the shout
      Of the Free rings out,
  And swells from shore to shore!

Sprung from the race of yoemen, their country's
    boast and pride,
His stalwart form has brav'd the storms that
    lash the mountain's side,
His manly forehead dripping with the sweat of
    honest toil,
As side by side by side he labor'd with the tillers
    of the soil.

Hurrah! hurrah! for honest Abe, hurrah! &c.

At eve, from toil returning, nought could his
 ardor damp—
To pore o'er Learning mysteries, he trims the
 midnight lamp ;
The syren-voice of Pleasure could not his youth
 enthrall,
No fetters bind the daring mind, no obstacles
 appall !

Hurrah ! hurrah ! for Honest Abe, hurrah ! &c.

Thus nobly has he struggled, and bravely bore
 the strife,
And proudly has he conquered, in the battle-
 field of life ;
From every hill and valley, the trumpet-voice
 of Fame
Rings out in loudest, clearest notes, our leader's
 spotless name !

Hurrah ! hurrah ! for Honest Abe, hurrah ! &c.

Come, freemen, join the chorus, raise high the
 swelling notes,
Like freemen give your suffrages—for Lincoln
 cast your votes !
Let " *Continental* " valor be " *Invincible* " in
 fight,
And " *Wide Awake* " to conquer, for Lincoln,
 Truth and Right.

Hurrah ! hurrah ! for Honest Abe, hurrah ! &c.

Honest Abe.

AIR—" *Few Days.* "

Old " Honest Abe " we will elect,
 In a few days—few days,
The Loco-focos we'll eject,
 And send Buchanan home.

CHORUS—For we will wait no longer,
    Than a few days, a few days,
    For we can wait no longer,
    To send Buchanan home.

Buchanan is in great distress,
    These few days—few days,
His grief he scarcely can express
    Because he's going home.
CHORUS—For we will wait no longer, &c.

ABE LINCOLN will be President,
    In a few days—few days,
To him the People will present,
    Buchanan's southern home.
CHORUS—For we will wait no longer, &c..

November it is near at hand,
    In a few days, few days,
The people then throughout the land
    Will send "OLD JIMMY" home.
CHORUS—For they will wait no longer, &c.

The people they are not afraid,
    In a few days—few days,
To take for Vice, with "Honest Abe"
    A man from Maine, his home.
CHORUS—For they will wait no longer, &c.

Then shout for ABE of Illinois,
    For a few days—few days,
For HAMLIN too your lungs employ,
    For they shan't stay at home.
CHORUS—For we will wait no longer, &c.

The fourth of March will soon be here,
    In a few days—few days,
The time for "Honest Abe" is near,
    To enter his new home.
.CHORUS—For we will wait no longer, &c.

For Lincoln and for Hamlin too,
  For a few days—few days,
We'll work with hearts who're ever true,
  To those they love at home.

CHORUS—For we will wait no longer, &c.

And when the vict'ry has been won
  In a few days—few days,
And ABE is safe in Washington,
  His Presidential Home.

CHORUS—Then we need wait no longer,
    Than a few days—few days,
  Then we need wait no longer,
    For happy times at home.

In the Days of True Democracy!

TUNE—"*In the days when we went Gypseying.*"

In the days of true Democracy
  A long time ago.
When Jefferson was in the van,
  And boldly met the foe,
Men fought for Freedom gallantly,
  (The same was not a sham,)
And Slav'ry was forbid to curse
  The farm of "Uncle Sam."
But now those glorious days are past,
  The "Party" sinks so low,
How altered from its palmy days
  A long time ago.

      How altered from, &c.

When Washington was President,
  A long time ago ;
The great North-West was Freedom's own,
  Forever to be so.

No " Border Ruffians " cursed her soil,
    Sustained by Federal tools—
No " Squatter Sovereigns " then were bred
    In democratic schools.
The love of Freedom was no crime,
    For which men's blood did flow
In the days of true Democracy,
    A long time ago.

       In the days of true, &c.

Those glorious days are now gone by,
    How altered are the times !
When office is securely held
    By foul official crimes.
A Sheriff's Posse now can strike
    The innocent and free—
And Marshals arm a bloody mob
    By Government decree.
Could tyrants thus have ruled our land,
    And ordered all things so,
In the days of true Democracy
    A long time ago?

       In the days of true, &c.

In the days of our first President,
    A long time ago—
When Slavery was condemned to die,
    And Freedom bid to grow,
We coveted no other lands,
    Nor islands in the sea—
No Filibuster diplomats
    Did represent the free.
No " Conference " of Buccaneers,
    To all the world did show
Democracy an empty name,
    A long time ago.

       Democracy an empty, &c.

Campaign Song.

BY DR. CHAS. POTTINGER.

[Dedicated to the "Continentals."]

AIR—"*Little Wee Man.*"

What has caused this great commotion,
  Motion, motion, motion,
    All the country through,
It is the ball that's rolling on,
For Honest Old Abe and Hamlin, too.

CHORUS.

For with them we can beat any man,
Of the Loco-foco clan,
For with them we can beat any man.

From rugged Maine to Mexico, co, co,
  From Illinois to California, too,
    We'll keep this ball a'rolling on,
    For Honest Old Abe and Hamlin, too,
      CHORUS, For with them, &c.

The North and South, and East and West,
    West, West,
  To the Union ever true,
Will help to roll the ball along,
  For Honest Old Abe and Hamlin, too.
    CHORUS, For with them, &c.

And when, at length, at Washington, ton, ton,
  The White House full in view,
We'll ne'er regret the battles won,
  For Honest Old Abe and Hamlin, too,
    CHORUS, For with them, &c.

So, here's to the noble patriots, patriots,
  Whose hearts, both brave and true,
Will help to roll the ball along,
  For honest Old Abe and Hamlin, too.
    CHORUS, For with them, &c.

The Flat-Boat Excursion.

AIR—" *We're bound to win.*"

Ho! patriots and friends of Freedom every-
    where,
Accept an invitation to go to Freedom's fair,
Aboard the jolly flat-boat as along the shore she
    rolls,
O! come, O! come, my merry boys, with oars
    and shoulder polls.

Abe Lincoln is our Captain, and Hamlin is our
    mate,
They'll point the way to triumph, as they guide
    the ship of state :
They'll lead the way to Freedom, in the road our
    fathers trod,
Their motto is the Union, our Country and our
    God.

And now along the verdant banks, our gallant
    captain steers,
While the clarion notes of Freedom's voice salute
    our listening ears ;
With our banners to the mast head, and our
    colors to the wind,
We'll start on our excursion and leave our foes
    behind.

We'll leave the artful dodger, sometimes called
    the "little giant,"
And all supple politicians with consciences so
    pliant ;
That in the South they'll flatter with oily
    tongued oration,
While in the North their motto is "unfriendly
    legislation.

6

We'll leave them and their platform—mysterious
    and unmeaning,
With an appetite for spoils so unquenched and
    overweaning :
That to keep their present places, by way of ab-
    solution,
To the South they offer Kansas—the Lecompton
    Constitution.

We'll leave them in the vassalage of territorial
    ties,
Of squatter rights, and Mormon rites, and
    slavery's subsides ;
We'll leave them in the quicksands of anti-home
    protection,
To honest art and handicraft, throughout each
    northern section,

We'll leave them in the hot-bed of bribery and
    plunder,
For we do not fear their threatenings, to rend
    the States asunder ;
So come on, my brave parties, come and join us
    everywhere,
And we'll send our honest Lincoln to the Presi-
    dent's chair.   ALDINE.

Campaign Song.

AIR—"*Star Spangled Banner.*"

O, say what is this that has caused such emo-
    tion,
From hamlet to hamlet, from ocean to ocean,
From New England's bright valleys, baptized by
    clear fountains,
Where the lofty pine waves from their beautiful
    mountains,

Where the laurel and ivy round her rocks doth
    entwine,
Where Liberty's air every heart doth enshrine?
'T is the fires of Freedom—and long may they
    glow
Where the evergreen waves over mantles of
    snow.

From the globes of the West where the wood-
    man's axe sounds,
Where the giant oak monarch the dense forest
    crowns,
Where the wolf, and the deer, and the antelope
    roam,
'T is there the bold pioneer seeks a new home.
There nurtured to Freedom in heaven's pure air,
Thus he lifts up his voice in the accents of
    prayer :
" May the curse of a tyrant or Slavery's chain
Ne'er pollute my fair State or dishonor her
    name."

Where the soft zephyrs play o'er the prairie
    ocean,
There, there doth humanity plight her devotion
To Freedom's own temple, bright temple of
    Fame,
There thousands of voices shout forth her loved
    name,
There LINCOLN the Honest, our LINCOLN the
    Brave,
Has raised the proud standard our country to
    save,
The Union is dear to Kentucky's own son ;
The Union, the Union, eternal in one. ALDINE.

Rail Lyric.

Air—"*Lord Lovel.*"

Judge Douglas he stood by the White House
  door,
  Asking for leave to go in ;
The Goddess of Liberty barred the way,
  As an Angel resisting sin,—sin,—sin,
    As an Angel resisting sin.

And who are you, little man, she said,
  And what have you done, said she ;
That you should have leave to enter here,
  To the house we hold for the free,—free,—free,
    To the house we hold for the free.

O ! I am a Giant, the little man cried,
  The terror of all the free ;
I murdered that innocent Compromise,
  And I'm fighting for sla-vee-ree,—ree,—ree,
    I'm fighting for sla-ve-ree.

The Goddess of Liberty shook her fist.
  And swore by the Augean stable ;
That there was no room for any one there,
  But the man, whose name was Abe—Abe—Abe,
    But the man, whose name was Abe–L.

Campaign Song.

Air—"*Wait for the Wagon.*"

Come, all ye friends of Freedom,
  And rally in each State,
For Honest Old Abe Lincoln,
  The people's candidate !
With Lincoln as our champion,
  We'll battle for the Right,
And beat the foes of Freedom,
  In next November's fight.

CHORUS—Hurrah ! boys, for Lincoln !
Hurrah ! boys, for Lincoln !
Hurrah ! boys, for Lincoln !
Hurrah ! for Hamlin, too !

The people want an honest man—
They're tired of fools and knaves ;
They're sick of imbecile "J. B.,"
That in the White House raves.
They want a man for President
Of firm, unyielding will,
That is both honest, brave and true,
And OLD ABE fills that bill !
CHORUS—Hurrah ! boys, &c.

Old Fogies down at Baltimore
In solemn conclave met,
The "Union-Saving" farce to play,
With Bell and Everett.
But the people, next November
Will put them all to rout,
And make them long remember
That the Fillmore game's "played out."
CHORUS—Hurrah ! boys, &c.

The Democrats are in a "fix,"
No wonder that they shiver ;
For they all feel it in their bones,
That they're going up Salt River !
With their party split asunder,
The truth is plain to all,
That though united once they stood,
Divided, now, they fall !
CHORUS—Hurrah ! boys, &c.

Oh, Douglas, you can't win this race,
You'd better clear the way—
Your humbug doctrines won't go down ;
At home you'll have to stay.
6*

The Wide-Awakes are on the march
  O'er all our hills and vales—
Our Giant-Killer's after you,
  With one of those old rails!
        CHORUS—Hurrah! boys, &c.

And Breckenridge will soon find out
  The people he can't fool;
They've had enough, these last four years,
  Of Democratic rule.
But LINCOLN is their favorite,
  And he is bound to win,—
When Buck steps out, next Fourth of March,
  OLD ABE will then step in!
        CHORUS—Hurrah! boys, &c,

Vive la Abe Lincoln.

BY CHARLES LEIB.

TUNE.—"*Vive la Companie.*"

Let us give three cheers for the man we love best,
        Vive la Abe Lincoln;
The son of Kentucky, Old Abe of the West,
        Vive la Abe Lincoln;
Protection and Freedom our watchwords shall be,
        Vive la Abe Lincoln;
Land for the landless! and homes for the free!
        Vive la Abe Lincoln!

  CHORUS:
      Vive la, vive la, vive la vive!
      Vive la, vive la, vive la vive!
      Vive la vive, vive la vive!
      Vive la Abe Lincoln!

The people are moving—have roused in their
      might;
        Vive la Abe Lincoln!

Their shout has gone forth for justice and right,
        Vive la Abe Lincoln !
They've sworn that Columbia, our dear land
    shall be,
        Vive la Abe Lincoln !
The land of the brave, and the home of the free,
        Vive la Abe Lincoln !
    CHORUS ;—Vive la, &c.

The men of the north, the true sons of toil,
        Vive la Abe Lincoln !
Advocate free men, free speech and free soil ;
        Vive la Abe Lincoln !
Their fathers were patriots, tried, true and brave,
        Vive la Abe Lincoln !
They fought for our freedom, they scorned the
    word slave,
        Vive la Abe Lincoln !
    CHORUS :—Vive la, &c.

Let the chorus ring out—the Union shall be,
        Vive la Abe Lincoln !
United forever—forever be free !
        Vive la Abe Lincoln !
Fire eaters may threaten, fanatics may rave,
        Vive la Abe Lincoln !
Our land shall be free—be the home of the brave,
        Vive la Abe Lincoln !
    CHORUS :—Vive la, &c.

Abe Lincoln to freedom has ever been true,
        Vive la Abe Lincoln !
And so has our Hamlin, the gallant, been too ;
        Vive la Abe Lincoln !
Up, up with our banner, make the welkin ring,
        Vive la Abe Lincoln !
We'll shout, we'll rejoice, and we'll joyfully sing,
        Vive la Abe Lincoln !
    CHORUS :—Vive la, &c.

Song of the Free.

AIR—"*Auld Lang Syne.*"

We come, we come, in joy we come,
  To fight the fight of Truth ;
From hoary head of wisdom sage
  To fiery crest of youth !

CHORUS.

Hurrah ! Hurrah ! there is no law
  To claim a freeman's soul ;
" The Constitution and the Right,"
  Our watchword—let it roll !

The land that God has given us,
  Is Freedom's cradle-home ;
And slavery shall not be allowed
  O'er more free soil to roam.

CHORUS.—Hurrah ! &c.

With Lincoln at our army's head
  We'll firmly meet the foe ;
And Freedom's song we'll e'er prolong,
  Ho ! brother-battlers, ho !

CHORUS.—Hurrah ! &c.

Campaign Song.

BY FRANCIS C WOODWORTH.

AIR—" *Sparkling and Bright.*"

Hear, freemen all,
  Your country's call,
And round our standard rally !
  Come, join our band,
  With heart and hand,
From every hill and valley !

CHORUS—When freedom's at stake
   Let the people awake!
  Their forces be set in motion,
   Let Lincoln's pure name
   In jubilant strain
  Be echoed from ocean to ocean.

   Let slavery remain
   Within the domain,
  Defined by the voice of our sages!
   But oh! let it spoil
   No more of the soil
  Devoted to freedom for ages!

CHORUS—When freedom's at stake, &c.

   We've truth on our side;
   We've God for our guide;
  Our cause is the cause of the nation;
   We'll never say *fail*;
   We're sure to prevail,
  And firmly we take our station!

CHORUS—When freedom's at stake, &c.

God and the Right.

AIR—"*America.*"

Sons of our northern land,
Of the old patriot band,
  Rouse for the fight,
Ready to "do or die."
Ring out your battle cry
Lincoln and Victory,
God and the right.

Sons of those sires who brought
Old England's sons to naught,
    By land and sea,
Uphold your country's fame !
Stain not her glorious name
With Slavery's deeds of shame—
    Dare to be free.

Stand for your Western plains
Crimsoned with martyr stains,
    Plant now your feet,
Yield not a single rood,
You need not be subdued ;
Stand as your fathers stood,
    Sound no retreat

Follow your leader on !
The fair West's chosen son
    Leads in the fight.
Fling your proud flag on high,
Ring out your battle cry, .
Lincoln and victory,
    God and the Right.

————

CONTENTS.

Page

Honest Abe of the West—"*Star Spangled Banner*" - - - - - 5
Rail Song—"*Dandy Jim*" - - - 6
Up again for the Conflict—"*Old Oaken Bucket*" 7
Hurrah for Old Abe of the West—"*Vive la companie*" - - - - - 9
Campaign Song—"*Rosin the Bow*" - - 11
Hail to our Chief—"*Hail to the Chief*" - 12
Old Abe—"*Ald Lang Syne*" - - - 13
People's Campaign Song—"*Nelly Gray*" - 15
Freedom and Reform—"*We're a band of Brothers*" - - - - - - 17
Hurrah Song. - - - - - - 17
Lincoln and Liberty—"*Hazel Dell*" - 20
Campaign Song—"*Constitution and Guerriere*" 21
Our glorious Constitution—"*Tullochgorum*" 22
Lincoln is the Word—"*Scots wha hæ*" - 24
Lincoln the Hope of the Nation—"*Columbia, the gem of the Ocean*" - - - - 25
Fourth of July Lincoln and Hamlin Song— "*Heart and Lute*" or, "*Auld Lang Syne*" 26
Dug was once a little man—"*Love was once a little boy*" - - - - - - 27
Stevy Dug—"*Uncle Ned*" - . - 28
Song of the Freemen—"*The Campbells are coming*" - - - - - 29
Clear the way—'*Home Again*" - - 30
Campaign Song to the Wide-Awakes of Philadelphia—"*Yankee Doodle*" - - 31
The "Continental" Refrain—"*Ho! Boys, carry me 'long*" - - - - - 33
Campaign Song—"*Dixey's Land*" - 34
Campaign Song—"*Araby's Daughter*" - 36

Old Abe's Preliminary Visit to the White
  House—"*Villikens and Dinah*"   -   - 37
John Anderson my Jo, John.   -   -   - 40
Lincoln and Hamlin Song—"*Nothing else to
  do*"   -   -   -   -   -   -   - •42
Lincoln and Liberty—"*Scots wha hæ wi Wal-
  lace bled*"   -   .   -   - 42
Abe of Illinois—"*Auld Lang Syne.*"   - 44
Abe Lincoln comes—"*Greeting Glee*"   - 44
Campaign Song—"*New Jer-se-a*"   -   - 46
The Restoration Party's Song—"*The Old
  Granite State*"   -   -   -   -   - 48
Faith and Trust—"*Zion*"   -   -   - 48
Anti-Party Glee—"*I once was Fond of a Social
  Glass*"   -   -   -   -   -   - 49
I spurn the Bribe—"*Mountains Farewell*" . 50
Campaign Song—"*Auld Lang Syne*"   - 51
God made us free—"*America*"   -   - 52
"Yaller Kiver" Melody—"*Rosin the Bow.*" 53
Campaign Song—"*Hurrah Chorus*"   - - 54
Campaign Song—"*Dearest Mae*"   -   - 55
Honest Abe—"*Few Days*"   -   -   - 56
In the Days of True Democracy—"*In the days
  when we went Gypseying*"   -   •   - 58
Campaign Song—"*Little Wee Man*"   - 60
The Flat-Boat Excursion—"*We're bound to
  win*"   -   -   -   -   -   - 61
Campaign Song—"*Star Spangled Banner*" 62
Rail Lyric—"*Lord Lovel*"   .   -   - 64
Vive la Abe Lincoln—"*Vive la Companie*" 66
Song of the Free—"*Auld Lang Syne*"   - 68
Campaign Song—"*Sparkling and Bright*" 68
God and the Right—"*America*"   -   - 69